Science Fair Workshop

by Marcia Daab

Fearon Teacher Aids
Simon & Schuster Supplementary Education Group

Editor: Carol Williams
Design and illustration: Rose Sheifer
Cover design and illustration: Sally Cox

ISBN 0-8224-6374-1

Printed in the United States of America
1. 9 8 7 6 5 4 3 2 1

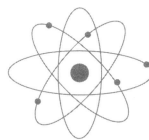

To the teacher . . .

Tackling a research-type science project seems like an impossible task to many students. They are often confused about where to begin and how to see the project through to completion. This step-by-step science project guide is designed to be reproduced so that each student will have a personal workbook. The project guide begins with a time line, so students can appropriately manage their time and set realistic goals. The guide is divided into seven clearly defined steps to make the science project process understandable to students. This programmed approach provides explanations and "how to" examples, as well as pages for recording information and observations. Since the amount of data each student gathers will vary, you might want to provide more than one copy of the pages that students will use to record their research (pages 12–14) and experiment observations (pages 33–37).

This is a step-by-step guide written especially for you—the student/scientist faced with the challenge of creating a research-type science fair project.

Your workbook clearly outlines seven essential steps you will need to follow to complete your project.

Before beginning with step one, use the time line on page 2 and make a schedule to determine a time allotment for each step, so that you can estimate when your final project will be completed.

The Time Line

Make a schedule for yourself. It will keep you on task at a reasonable rate and help eliminate a last-minute rush. Generally four to eight weeks should be plenty of time to complete a project.

Today's date: _____

Due Dates

Brainstorm (2 days)
• Choose topic

_____

Research (1 week)
• Identify research variables
• Gather information
• Write bibliography
• Write hypothesis

_____

Experiment
• Write procedure
• Identify all variables $\Big\}$ (2 days)
• Gather materials
• Conduct experiment (3 days–2 weeks)

_____

Record Results (2 days)
• Write observations
• Prepare graphs and charts

_____

Draw Conclusions (2 days)

_____

Write Report (2–4 days)

_____

Prepare Exhibit (2–4 days)

_____

Dates of:
Local Science Fair

_____

District Science Fair

_____

Regional Science Fair

_____

Science Fair Workshop © 1990 Fearon Teacher Aids

BRAINSTORM

Topical Storm (**täp-i-kəl stôrm**) *n* a violent out-break of ideas for your science fair project. This storm occurs in various areas. Its energy blows and whirls your interests and experiences around, creating a blinding list of project topics.

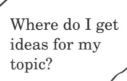

Where do I get ideas for my topic?

Famous Topical Storm Areas

1. Your interests or hobbies
2. Teacher suggestions
3. Science class topics
4. Parents, relatives, and friends
5. Library
6. TV

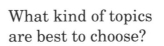

What kind of topics are best to choose?

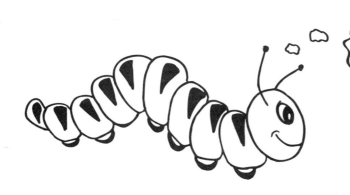

Be sure your topic can be tested. Topics such as space and planets are good to research, but it would be difficult to set up an experiment to test your research. Keep in mind that you will be researching your topic and then setting up an experiment to test your hypothesis. If you keep this process in mind, it will help you choose appropriate topics.

Science Fair Workshop © 1990 Fearon Teacher Aids

Ready? Go!

List a flurry of topics that you have an interest in and would be suitable for a science fair project.

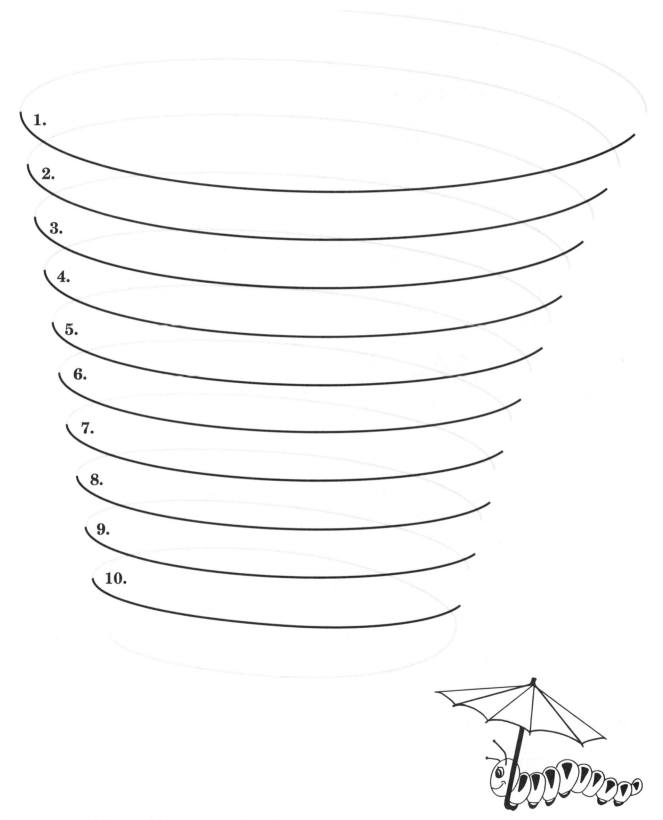

1.

2.

3.

4.

5.

6.

7.

8.

9.

10.

The purpose is . . .
Getting to the Point
Narrow Your Topic

1. List the relationships that are found within the topic area.

   For example, in the area of plants there are the relationships between plants and water, plants and sunlight, plants and fertilizer, and plants and temperature. All of these relationships are testable because one affects the other.

2. After you have established a relationship for the topic, ask a question about the relationship. The question should point out a **cause and effect,** which will be the purpose of your experiment.

   For example, if the relationship between plants and fertilizers is chosen, this question could be asked, Will fertilizer "x" or "y" cause petunias to grow taller?

Here is a sample chart of topics, topic relationships, and questions.

Topics	Topic Relationships	Questions
Plants	plants and fertilizers	Will fertilizer "x" or "y" **cause** petunias to grow taller?
Weather temperature	weather temperature and insulation	Can insulation **cause** an ice cube to melt at a slower rate?
Friction	friction and rolling	Can surface texture **cause** a change in my skateboard speed?

   Science Fair Workshop © 1990 Fearon Teacher Aids

Get to the Point

Practice narrowing some of the topics you listed on page 5.

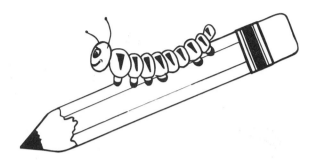

Topics	Topic Relationships	Questions
1. _____	_____	_____
	_____	_____
		_____
2. _____	_____	_____
	_____	_____
3. _____	_____	_____
	_____	_____
		_____
4. _____	_____	_____
	_____	_____
		_____

Choose a question from page 7 that you want to investigate and write it here.

_____

_____

_____

_____

_____

Remember . . .

Your question should show a cause and effect. Check to see if yours does.

- The **cause** is something that can be changed or manipulated. It is also called the **independent variable.**
- The **effect** is the result of the cause. It is also called the **dependent variable.**

     Science Fair Workshop © 1990 Fearon Teacher Aids

RESEARCH

Now it's time to find out as much about your topic as you can. This will help you decide what you think the answer to your question might be.

SOURCES OF INFORMATION

Places	People	Literature
school	teacher	science books
library	librarian	project books
home	family/friends	encyclopedias
businesses	doctor/dentist	magazines
garden center	veterinarian	newspapers
zoo	scientist	yellow pages

Identify the Variables

Before you can begin your research, you need to identify the variables in your question. Both variables, the **independent** and the **dependent,** need to be researched.

Remember, the **cause** is the **independent variable** and the **effect** is the **dependent variable.**

Here are some samples:

Will fertilizer "x" or "y" cause petunias to grow taller?
independent variable: fertilizers "x" and "y"
dependent variable: growth of petunias

Can insulation cause an ice cube to melt at a slower rate?
independent variable: insulation
dependent variable: rate at which an ice cube melts

Can surface texture cause a change in skateboard speed?
independent variable: surface texture
dependent variable: skateboard speed

Restate your question from page 8 and identify the variables.

_____

_____

independent variable: _____

dependent variable: _____

Science Fair Workshop © 1990 Fearon Teacher Aids

Plot Your Path

List the variables you identified on page 10 and decide which resource materials you will use to research each variable.

Here is an example:

Sources

Independent Variable: fertilizers "x" and "y"	garden center, nursery worker, plant or fertilizer books
Dependent Variable: growth of petunias	garden center, nursery worker, encyclopedia, library

Sources

Independent Variable:	
Dependent Variable:	

In Your Own Words, Please!

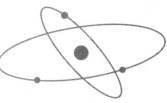

Write down all the important facts about your **independent variable.**

_____

_____

_____

_____

_____

_____

_____

_____

_____

_____

_____

_____

_____

_____

Where did you get this information?

_____

Person's name   Occupation

Or

_____

Author   Title

_____

City of publication   Publisher   Volume/Page numbers

_____

Copyright date

More Words . . .

Write down all the important facts about your **dependent variable.**

_____

_____

_____

_____

_____

_____

_____

_____

_____

_____

_____

_____

_____

Where did you get this information?

_____

Person's name   Occupation

Or

_____

Author   Title

_____

City of publication   Publisher   Volume/Page numbers

_____

Copyright date

And More . . .

Write down all the information that helps explain how the two variables are related.

_____

_____

_____

_____

_____

_____

_____

_____

_____

_____

_____

_____

_____

Where did you get this information?

_____

Person's name   Occupation

Or

_____

Author   Title

_____

City of publication   Publisher   Volume/Page numbers

_____

Copyright date

                            Science Fair Workshop © 1990 Fearon Teacher Aids

Put It All Together

Now put the information you have gathered on pages 12–14 together into a complete report. Include background information on both variables and the relationship between them. Be sure to include how you think this information is valuable to others.

_____

_____

_____

_____

_____

_____

_____

_____

_____

_____

_____

_____

_____

_____

_____

_____

_____

_____

_____

_____

_____

_____

Science Fair Workshop © 1990 Fearon Teacher Aids

What Is a Bibliography?

A bibliography is an alphabetical list of all the books, magazines, pamphlets, newspapers, or people that you used in researching your topic and writing your report.

Here are some samples to follow:

People

Last name, first name. Occupation. Address: Date contacted.

Smith, Bob. Gardener. 2801 North 5th, St. Louis, MO 63001: November 28, 1987.

Books

Author's last name, first name. (copyright date). <u>Title of book</u>. City of publication: Publisher.

Flower, John. (1986). <u>How to Grow Petunias</u>. Boston: Webster Printing Company.

Magazines

Author's last name, first name. (year published, month). Title of article. <u>Title of magazine</u>, page numbers.

Plant, Alice. (1986, July). How Fertilizers Help Plants. <u>Botanical Journal</u>, pp. 12–14.

List your bibliography entries alphabetically.

Science Fair Workshop © 1990 Fearon Teacher Aids

Write Your Hypothesis

You've already done the hard part—deciding on a topic, narrowing it, and researching it. Now, decide how you think your question on page 8 should be answered. Change the question to an "If/then" statement. This statement is called the **hypothesis.**

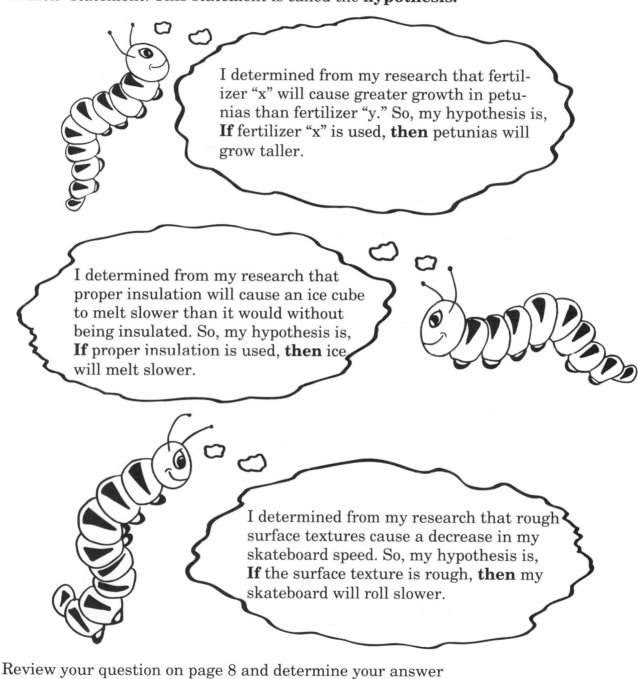

I determined from my research that fertilizer "x" will cause greater growth in petunias than fertilizer "y." So, my hypothesis is, **If** fertilizer "x" is used, **then** petunias will grow taller.

I determined from my research that proper insulation will cause an ice cube to melt slower than it would without being insulated. So, my hypothesis is, **If** proper insulation is used, **then** ice will melt slower.

I determined from my research that rough surface textures cause a decrease in my skateboard speed. So, my hypothesis is, **If** the surface texture is rough, **then** my skateboard will roll slower.

Review your question on page 8 and determine your answer based on your research. Write your hypothesis.

If _____

then _____

EXPERIMENT

To determine if your hypothesis is correct, you need to conduct a simple experiment. The step-by-step directions for this experiment are called the **procedure.** The **procedure** is like a recipe. You need to tell times, sizes, amounts, and in what order each step is to be done.

Use metric measurements in your **procedure.**

To Measure:	Use:
Width / Length / Height	millimeters (mm) centimeters (cm) meters (m) kilometers (km)
Mass	grams (g) kilograms (kg)
Volume 100 ml	milliliters (ml) liters (l) kiloliters (kl)

The Variables

Before setting up your experiment you must be aware of all the variables. You have already identified two of the four variables—**independent** and **dependent.** Now you must consider the remaining two variables.

The **constant variables**

are those things that you must keep the same, so the experiment will be a fair test. If an experiment were set up to test if fertilizer "x" really did cause petunias to grow taller, then the variables such as pot size, amounts of sunlight, and amounts of water must remain constant. If only the **independent variable,** which in this case is the fertilizer, is changing, then it will be a fair test of that variable's effects.

The **control**

is the absence of the **independent variable.** In the case of the petunias, a plant would have to be grown without fertilizer to compare it to the growth of a plant that had been fertilized. In the case of the insulation, an ice cube would have to be tested to see how fast it melts without insulation to compare the results with the melting speed of an insulated ice cube.

- Keep these two variables in mind as you write the **procedure** for your experiment.

Plan the Procedure

The **procedure** for your experiment is like a recipe. Be precise and write each direction on a new line. Don't worry about the exact order now, but be specific.

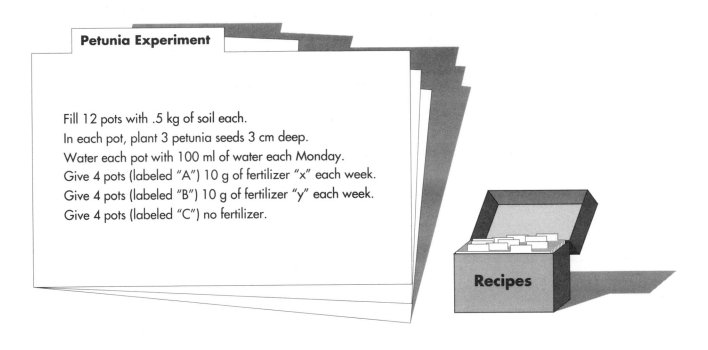

Petunia Experiment

Fill 12 pots with .5 kg of soil each.
In each pot, plant 3 petunia seeds 3 cm deep.
Water each pot with 100 ml of water each Monday.
Give 4 pots (labeled "A") 10 g of fertilizer "x" each week.
Give 4 pots (labeled "B") 10 g of fertilizer "y" each week.
Give 4 pots (labeled "C") no fertilizer.

Recipes

Notice in the sample that 12 pots of petunia plants were used. Be sure you use enough test items in your experiment or repeat the experiment three times.

_____

_____

_____

_____

_____

_____

_____

_____

_____

   Science Fair Workshop © 1990 Fearon Teacher Aids

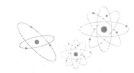

Procedure Check

Before going any further, check over your **procedure** on pages 22–23. Identify the following four variables to be sure your "recipe" will be a fair test of your hypothesis.

1. What is the **independent variable** (IV)?

_____

_____

2. What is the **dependent variable** (DV)?

_____

_____

3. What are the **constant variables** (CV)?

_____

_____

_____

4. What is the **control?**

_____

_____

_____

Did you use metric measurements?

Science Fair Workshop © 1990 Fearon Teacher Aids

The Final Recipe

After you have carefully identified your variables and have made sure you have included each necessary step in your experiment, cut apart the directions on pages 22–23. Glue them below in the correct order and then number each direction.

_____

_____

_____

_____

_____

_____

_____

_____

_____

_____

_____

_____

_____

_____

_____

_____

_____

Materials List

Make a complete list of all of the items you will need to conduct your experiment.

1. _____
2. _____
3. _____
4. _____
5. _____
6. _____
7. _____
8. _____
9. _____
10. _____
11. _____
12. _____

Things I need:
1. petunia seeds
2. twelve 10 cm clay pots
3. 1 bag potting soil
4. 1 bag fertilizer "x"
5. 1 bag fertilizer "y"
6. measuring cup
7. water
8. newspaper

Ready . . .   **Gather the materials in your list.**

Set . . .   **Read the procedure.**

Go!   **Begin your experiment!**

Science Fair Workshop © 1990 Fearon Teacher Aids

RECORD RESULTS

It is important for you to keep accurate and organized data **while** conducting your experiment. Using logs and drawings, write down all observations and results during the entire time you are conducting your experiment (3 days–2 weeks). Use the 2 days set aside on your time line for "recording results" to organize your information into tables, charts, and graphs.

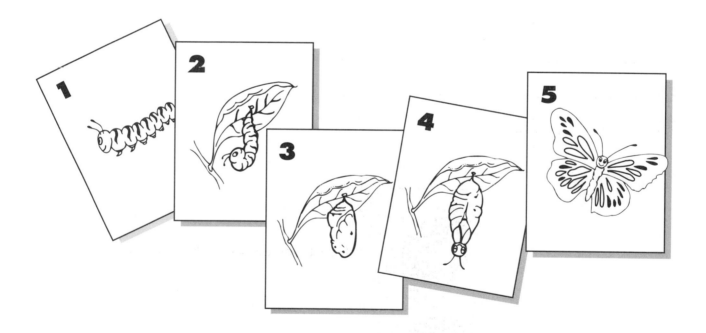

Data Table

A data table is a good way to show your experiment results in an organized way. Here is a data table that has been used to record the results of the plant growth in the petunia experiment. (The height of the tallest sprout was recorded for each group each week.)

PLANT GROWTH

	A (fertilizer "x")	B (fertilizer "y")	C (no fertilizer)
Week 1	3 cm	2 cm	2 cm
Week 2	6 cm	5 cm	5 cm
Week 3	10 cm	9 cm	7 cm
Week 4	13 cm	12 cm	10 cm
Totals	32 cm	28 cm	24 cm
Average	8 cm	7 cm	6 cm

Log

Use a log if your results and observations are in words. Record your results, using one page for each day.

Science Fair Workshop © 1990 Fearon Teacher Aids

Chart

Make a drawing or chart to describe your observed results.

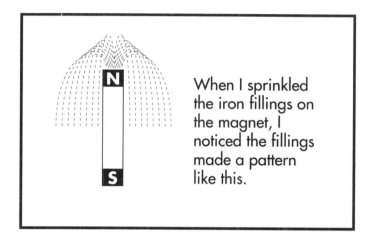

When I sprinkled the iron fillings on the magnet, I noticed the fillings made a pattern like this.

Graphs

A graph is another way to organize your data if the results are given in numbers. There are many types of graphs. Choose the one that presents your data most clearly.

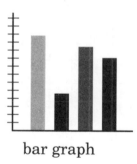

bar graph

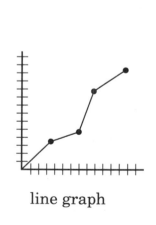

line graph

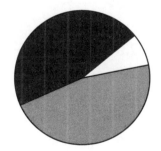

pie graph

Line Graph

Here is a sample line graph for the petunia experiment. Notice the vertical scale shows the height (in centimeters) of the **dependent variable** (petunias).

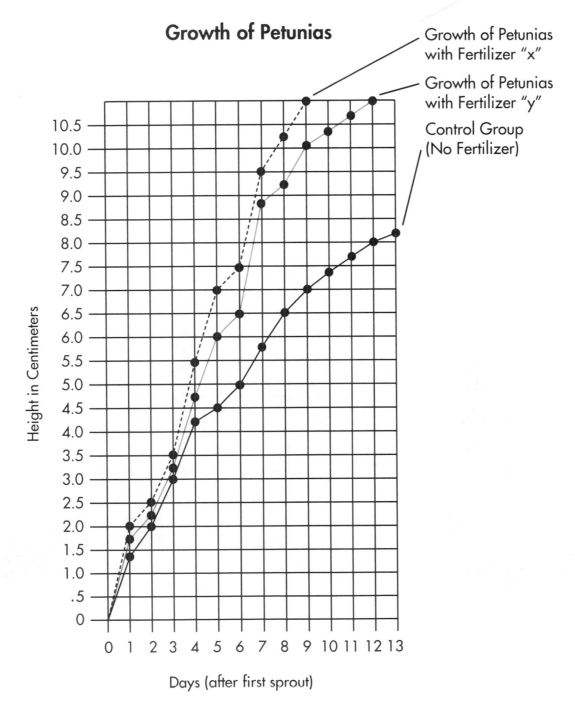

Growth of Petunias

Growth of Petunias
with Fertilizer "x"

Growth of Petunias
with Fertilizer "y"

Control Group
(No Fertilizer)

Height in Centimeters

10.5
10.0
9.5
9.0
8.5
8.0
7.5
7.0
6.5
6.0
5.5
5.0
4.5
4.0
3.5
3.0
2.5
2.0
1.5
1.0
.5
0

0 1 2 3 4 5 6 7 8 9 10 11 12 13

Days (after first sprout)

Science Fair Workshop © 1990 Fearon Teacher Aids

Bar Graph

Here is a sample bar graph for the petunia experiment. Again, the vertical scale represents the **dependent variable.** Notice also that both the vertical and horizontal scales should be labeled and the graph should have a title.

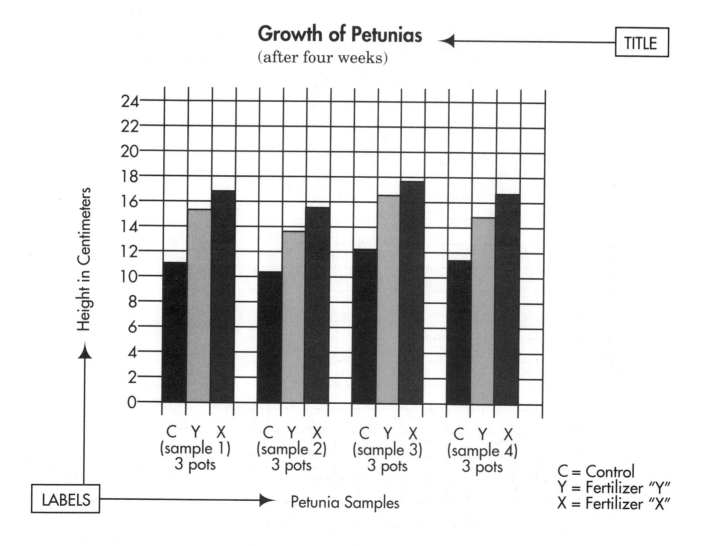

Growth of Petunias
(after four weeks)

TITLE

Height in Centimeters

24
22
20
18
16
14
12
10
8
6
4
2
0

C Y X
(sample 1)
3 pots

C Y X
(sample 2)
3 pots

C Y X
(sample 3)
3 pots

C Y X
(sample 4)
3 pots

C = Control
Y = Fertilizer "Y"
X = Fertilizer "X"

LABELS → Petunia Samples

Pie Graph

A pie graph is used to show how parts are compared to a whole. The petunia experiment results would not be represented appropriately with this type of graph. However, survey results are very clearly represented using a pie graph.

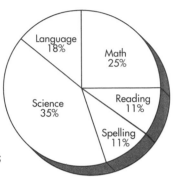

A class of 28 students was surveyed, and the students were asked to name their favorite school subject. Here are the results in a pie graph.

To make this pie graph, these simple steps were followed:

1

Survey students.

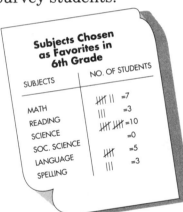

2

Calculate percentage. Divide the tally total for each subject by the total number of students surveyed.

Math $\cancel{||||}\ ||$ = 7

7/28 = .25 or 25%

3

Calculate degrees. Multiply the percent in decimal form by 360°.

.25 x 360° = 90°

Use the degrees to divide the pie circle.

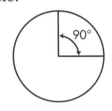

The data table shows an organized way to calculate and record this information:

Subjects	No. of Students	Calculation of Decimal Fraction	Calculation of Degrees
Math	7	7/28 = .25	.25 x 360° = 90°
Reading	3	3/28 = .11	.11 x 360° = 40°
Science	10	10/28 = .35	.35 x 360° = 126°
Soc. Studies	0	0/28 = .00	0 x 360° = 0°
Language	5	5/28 = .18	.18 x 360° = 64°
Spelling	3	3/28 = .11	.11 x 360° = 40°
TOTALS	28	1.00	360°

Write down your experiment observations here.

_____

_____

_____

_____

_____

_____

_____

_____

_____

_____

_____

_____

_____

_____

_____

_____

_____

Use this space to draw your experiment results.

Science Fair Workshop © 1990 Fearon Teacher Aids

Use these circles to make pie graphs.

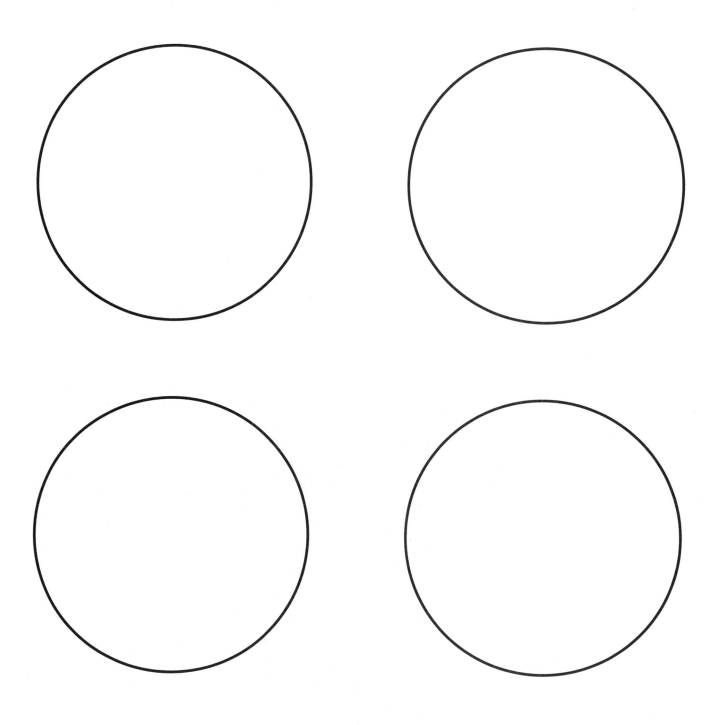

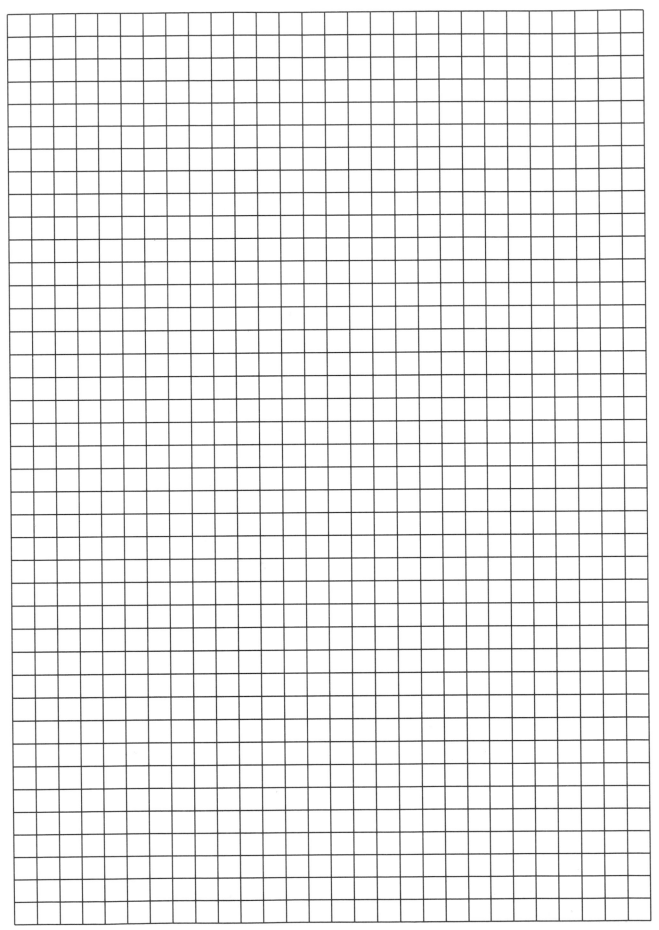

36

Use this page to make data tables or charts.

DRAW CONCLUSIONS

Conclusions are the ending to your story. Without conclusions your experiment is incomplete.

Your conclusions should

- tell in words exactly what happened during the experiment.

- tell whether your results supported your hypothesis.

- answer all questions that came up during the experiment.

- state any other information that was discovered in the process.

The End

Write Your Conclusions

Here are some sample conclusions from the petunia experiment.

The petunias fertilized with "x" grew 13 cm in 4 weeks. The petunias fertilized with "y" grew 12 cm in 4 weeks. The control, petunias with no fertilizer, grew 10 cm in 4 weeks. This data supports my hypothesis that petunias will grow taller with fertilizer "x." My experiment also shows that petunias grew taller with fertilizer "y" than with no fertilizer at all. This information would be important to nurseries selling petunias and fertilizers. Another question that might be investigated is whether plants other than petunias would have the same reaction to the two fertilizers.

WRITE REPORT

You must now organize all of your written information, charts, and graphs into a complete written report. What you have done so far is your rough draft. Before you begin to organize and rewrite the information, do this important three-point check:

✓ Check for correct spelling and grammar.

✓ Check for complete sentences and well-structured paragraphs.

✓ Check for accurate calculations.

The final copy of your report should be typed or rewritten very neatly in ink. (**Remember to acknowledge the typist in your report if you use one.**) Use the guide on the next page to help you organize your information in the correct order.

Science Fair Workshop © 1990 Fearon Teacher Aids

Organize Your Information

The first five pages of your report will look like this:

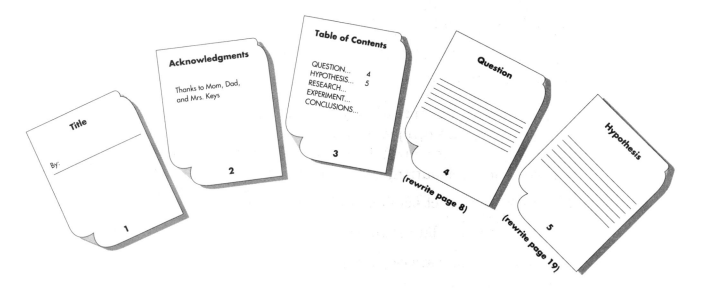

The rest of your report (pages 6 and following) will vary in page count, depending on the amount of material you have written and the number of graphs and charts you include. Put each of the following items on a new page in the order they are listed.

- Background information (rewrite pages 15–16)
- Experiment procedure (rewrite page 25)
- Variables (rewrite page 24)
- Materials list (rewrite page 26)
- Results (rewrite page 33)
- Graphs, charts, tables (rewrite pages 34–37)
- Conclusions (rewrite page 39)
- Bibliography (rewrite page 18)

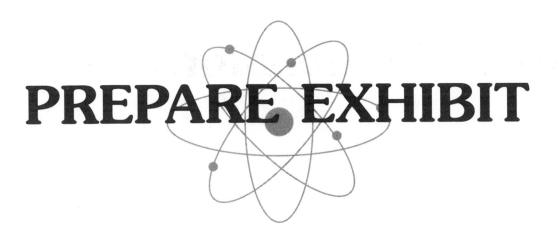

PREPARE EXHIBIT

Your exhibit is an attractive, well-organized display of all your hard work! Your exhibit can be designed in a variety of ways; however, there are some specific size guidelines that must be followed to enter your exhibit in the science fair. It is also very important that you use neat lettering and arrange your work in a clear, simple way.

Science Fair Workshop © 1990 Fearon Teacher Aids

Exhibit Dimensions

Here is a suggestion on how to arrange your work to make an attractive display.

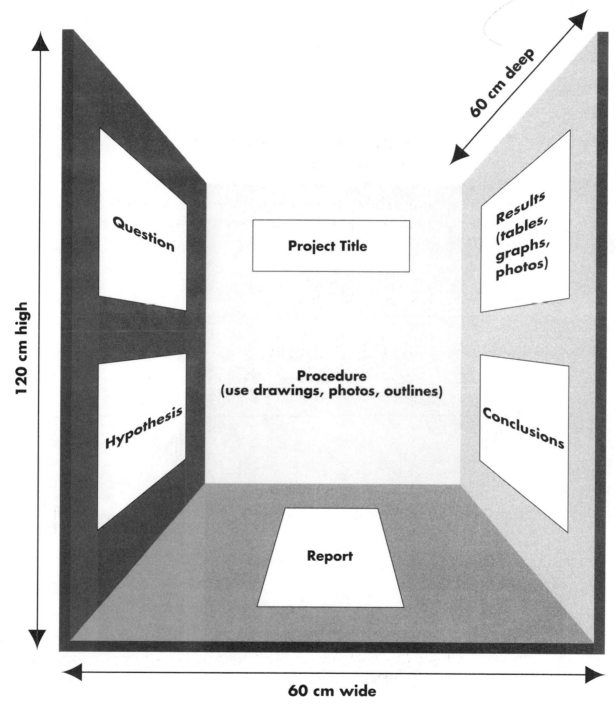

60 cm deep

120 cm high

Question

Project Title

Results (tables, graphs, photos)

Hypothesis

Procedure
(use drawings, photos, outlines)

Conclusions

Report

60 cm wide

All exhibits must be **no larger** than 60 cm deep, 60 cm wide, and 120 cm high. Use materials that are lightweight but sturdy enough for self-support.